THE VALUE OF BEING VALUABLE

THE VALUE OF BEING VALUABLE

CREATING MEANINGFUL
CONTENT THAT WILL WIN OVER
CUSTOMERS FOR LIFE

LEN MARKIDAN

COPYRIGHT © 2018 LEN MARKIDAN
All rights reserved.

THE VALUE OF BEING VALUABLE
Creating Meaningful Content That Will Win over Customers for Life

ISBN   978-1-5445-1068-2 *Paperback*
            978-1-5445-1069-9 *Ebook*

TABLE OF CONTENTS

INTRODUCTION: RISE ABOVE THE NOISE 9

1. IT'S ALL ABOUT VALUE 19
2. FIND OUT WHAT YOUR CUSTOMERS REALLY WANT 35
3. CREATE CONTENT THAT CONNECTS 57
4. GET YOUR MESSAGE TO YOUR MARKET 69
5. NURTURE YOUR AUDIENCE 83

CONCLUSION: THE PAY-OFF 105

ACKNOWLEDGMENTS 111

ABOUT THE AUTHOR 115

INTRODUCTION

RISE ABOVE THE NOISE

WHY CONTENT MARKETING?

Whenever I'm trying to drive home the importance of content marketing, I tell the story of a company called Groove, where I used to lead the marketing department. Seven years ago, Groove was a start-up that had just built a new type of customer service software. We did a lot of research and got plenty of feedback about our *product* before launching the business, but what we didn't have was a lot of *market* research. As a result, when our product hit the market, Groove hardly signed up any customers at all.

Groove launched a product that solved an important problem for people; managing customer service messages is complicated. Sure, the product wasn't perfect on day one, but it was good enough to be valuable. Unfortunately, not many people were paying for it. And, really, how *could* people pay for something they didn't know existed? In addition to not building a customer base ahead of time, we didn't do very much to market our new product at first. As if all that wasn't enough, we were also selling into a very crowded space with dozens of competitors, making it even more difficult to stand out.

Groove fell into the same trap a lot of companies fall into, which is the "if we build it, they will come" mentality. There is a belief out there that marketing isn't necessary: what really matters is building a great product that will speak for itself. We should all be putting good products on the market, but that's simply not enough in and of itself. You have to give people a reason to buy your product. But long before you can do that, you have to let people know that your company and your product exists. Your product *can't* speak for itself; *you* have to speak for it.

Let's think about this in the context of dating. Consider Sam, an imaginary young man who isn't having much luck with the ladies. Sam wears the same old T-shirt every day, hasn't had a haircut in months, and doesn't exercise. "I'm not going to bother taking care of myself," Sam declares. "Women should like me for who I am!" I'm sure we can all agree it would be wonderful to live in a world where everybody liked one another for what was on the inside. But the reality is that when a woman is swiping through dating apps that put thousands of potential matches at her fingertips, it's impossible for her to make her initial judgments based on what those choices are "like on the inside." Similarly, your potential customers are being barraged by a thousand marketing messages every day. How can they possibly judge your product based on what's inside? Or even *find* your product for that matter?

WHAT GOOD CONTENT MARKETING *ISN'T*

It's easy to see why, before long, Groove was about six months away from running out of cash. We had been mentioned in a couple of tech publications, but the resulting small bursts of traffic consisted of tire-kickers and unqualified leads who were unlikely to become paying customers. Soon, the traction these publications had brought us fizzled out, and we found ourselves back at square one.

In addition to these media hits, we had done a bit of blogging, along the lines of "Ten Reasons You Should Buy Our Product," and "Five Quotes from Business People about Customer Service." In other words, *really* bad content, which wasn't even remotely compelling or useful to our audience. We were publishing the textbook definition of what I've since come to call "checkbox content." We knew we *should* be doing content marketing, so we did it badly, just to check it off our list. Checkbox content marketing is a complete waste of time for reasons we'll get into in the pages to come.

Suffice it to say, Groove's blogging efforts didn't deliver the results we were looking for, and our website received no more than a couple hundred visitors per month—certainly not enough traffic to build a profitable business.

WHAT GOOD CONTENT MARKETING LOOKS LIKE

Like many other companies that started around 2010, Groove launched in the midst of a changing landscape. Social media marketing was just emerging, smartphones were becoming more and more engrained in our daily lives, and how people learned about products was in flux. We were part of this changing landscape, learning as we went.

Like all inflection points, this one took a lot of people on a roller-coaster ride, including Groove. Unfortunately, at first, it looked like we were well on our way to the same sad ending as thousands of other startups that died during this time, before their markets even knew them. During this period, we had a lot of discussions about how Groove could get from where we were to where we needed to be. We agreed we needed not just a marketing campaign, but a long-term reputable system for garnering leads and customers. We could see that a lot of tech companies were winning with content marketing, which seemed like a strategy that could work for Groove, too. We reached out to several successful tech companies and asked them questions such as, "What are you guys doing to succeed?" "What strategies are working really well for you?" "What hasn't worked so well for you?" "What do you wish you knew when you started?"

These conversations taught us that there were very sophisticated content-marketing strategies going on behind the scenes of these campaigns. Also, there were certain tactics these successful companies engaged in every single day.

It turned out that companies that were successful with their content-marketing strategies were striving to understand what their audience wanted, where their customers spent their time online, how they could get people to share their content, and how to nurture their e-mail subscribers, so they would evolve into customers.

For six weeks, we did nothing but talk—not only with successful content marketers who were willing to get on the phone, but with Groove's small customer base and people in our target audience. We asked what their biggest challenges were, and how we might help solve them. We got to the root of the real thorns in the side of small business founders and CEOs. Very rarely did anyone we talked with mention anything that had to do with customer service. It just wasn't something that kept these executives up at night.

Instead, our target audience was trying to find solutions for growth, marketing, hiring, and sales. *These* were the problems that kept them up at night. "Huh!" we thought. "Groove has exactly the same problems. Instead of writing about customer service, what if we write about our *own* experiences with these problems and how we're going about solving those challenges?" We decided to publish a new blog all about how we were tackling our marketing, growth, and hiring challenges. We showed companies in our customer base and target audience what things look like at another start-up—ours—that was experiencing the same problems and stressors they were experiencing. We wanted to be extremely relatable and extremely honest. We shared everything—our numbers, our wins *and* our fails, and all the different lessons we were learning along the way.

We launched a blog titled "A SaaS Start-up's Journey to $100,000 in Monthly Revenue." (SaaS stands for Software-as-a-Service.) We opened by explaining that we were at $28,000 per month in revenue right then, and we were going to blog about our journey to $100,000 in monthly revenue. We promised to share everything we learned and not to hold back, with the tagline "From 'aha' to 'oh, shit,' we're sharing everything on our journey to $100K in monthly revenue."

Within twenty-four hours, Groove's blog had 1,000 subscribers. Within a week, it had 5,000. Today, it has more than 100,000 subscribers and hosts more than a quarter-million visitors each month. More importantly, the blog quickly became—and, to this day, remains—their biggest driver of leads and sales.

Five years later, traffic and business have continued to grow substantially. Every year, Groove sets a new growth record. In 2017, the company did $5 million in sales. Although Groove has now expanded to two blogs—one about the start-up journey and one about customer service—as of this writing, Groove has never invested a dime in advertising. Content marketing remains their primary marketing channel.

"DIFFERENT" RESONATES

A large part of Groove's success has to do with the fact that we were doing something different with our start-up blog content. It's really easy to write a bland post about customer service or to say, "Here are ten success stories that will explain what you need to do with your business." It's easy to talk about your own wins, because it makes you look good. But it's a lot harder to find companies that provide a different, unique, and more thoughtful slant. Groove's willingness to do this made the company stand out in the eyes of our audience.

We built the blog we wished had existed when we needed answers—a place that would speak in our language, give us the advice we needed, and also serve as a voice of solidarity. Each company accomplishes this in its own way. In this book, you're going to figure out exactly what that way is for *your* company.

I've worked with dozens of companies to help them find their own unique way of connecting with customers through content. For every company, the specifics are different, but the process is always the same, whether it's a mom 'n' pop shop or a Fortune 500 company. It involves finding your market and your unique voice—neither of which can be done until you know who your customer is, what their problems are, and how they speak. This is how you get to the heart of providing value. And providing value *works*—for everyone.

CHAPTER ONE

IT'S ALL ABOUT VALUE

Have you ever seen someone smile and cringe simultaneously? You have if you've witnessed me hearing content marketing being called a "fad," which happens a lot. The cringe-smile is an odd look, but here's why I can't help it: I cringe, of course, because content marketing is my job. But I smile because calling it a fad is so, so wrong, and I have a story to prove it. Now I get to tell that story in a book, which is even better!

IS CONTENT MARKETING A FAD?

Just like most things digital, *digital* content marketing isn't anything new. In fact, content marketing itself has been around for hundreds of years; it's just the digital part of it that's novel. It even stretches back well before the example I'm about to share. But for now, we'll travel back about 130 years in time to when three brothers launched a start-up called Johnson & Johnson. Initially, their business focused on surgical dressings, like gauze. Today, we realize how important such products are. They prevent infection, keep our cuts and wounds clean, and stop our injuries from getting worse. But when Johnson & Johnson launched, these weren't universally accepted truths. In fact, in the 1880s, these ideas were controversial.

At the time, a British surgeon named Joseph Lister was researching antiseptic practices in surgery. He was among the early pioneers of antiseptic medicine and argued that we should try to protect open wounds from bacteria. In fact, he said, bacteria were causing dangerous infections in patients. It was so bad that some of these patients were dying from infections that started on the operating table. This was a real problem, but Lister's research had yet to be accepted by the mainstream.

To convince potential customers of the importance of their products in light of this new research, Johnson & Johnson crafted a piece of content marketing in its purest form. The company interviewed prominent, forward-thinking surgeons and doctors who agreed with Joseph Lister. Then, in 1888, they published a book called *Modern Methods of Antiseptic Wound Treatment*—a riveting read, I assure you—with insights from doctors about how Lister was on to something, and what protecting patients against infection would mean for the future of medicine. Very quickly, this book became the authority on what the future of surgery would look like. By providing this valuable information and offering a solution to people's problems, within six years, Johnson & Johnson was selling three-and-a-half million yards of gauze annually.

There was nothing more than a discreet nudge at the very end of the book that explained what Johnson & Johnson was and the products they were selling. This wasn't a book about why you should buy Johnson & Johnson's products. Rather, people *wanted* to buy from Johnson & Johnson because of the valuable information the book provided.

DELIVERING VALUE

In business, we tend to think it's our product that sets us apart from everyone else. As you can see from Johnson & Johnson, that's not the case. Great marketing won't save a poor product, but even great products will fail if nobody hears about them. What complicates this further is even if you do get your product in front of someone, very rarely will anyone buy from you the first time they hear about you.

Imagine you're selling accounting services. Not everybody is ready to buy accounting services today; in fact, *most* people probably aren't. However, the number of people who will need accounting services *at some point in the not-too-distant future* is exponentially higher. If you build trust, authority, and a relationship with this audience through content marketing, when the time comes for them to buy accounting services, you will be the first business they think of. After all, you've already delivered them so much value.

For example, an accounting firm might provide an ongoing series of videos that answer its target audience's Finance 101 questions, delivering value in the form of education. When the day comes for a viewer to purchase accounting services, this accounting firm is the natural choice; it's already the customer's go-to source for financial information.

The way to deliver value is to solve problems for people. I'm talking about much more than just the problem your specific product or service can solve—that comes later. In the meantime, people have no shortage of other problems, which your product probably *doesn't* solve and might not even have anything to do with! For example, the first start-up I worked with sold software to run A/B tests on websites. Today, this type of software is common and cheap, but it wasn't back then. We realized a lot of the chief marketing officers (CMOs) and marketing executives we wanted to sell to weren't thinking about A/B testing. They had other problems to contend with—problems with copy, design, management, and marketing strategy.

We started building content to solve those problems—

problems that had nothing to do with A/B testing software. For example: Should I have a money-back guarantee on my pricing page? Will that increase or decrease conversions? What's the optimal layout for a sales page? What are SEO best practices? Because our company had answers, people subscribed to our e-mail list. By the time the company was acquired, it had more than 4,000 paying customers.

In the next chapter, we'll get into specific strategies for doing this, but the bottom line is you need to understand what your customers' problems are and how you can solve those problems. If you can demonstrate and deliver that value, you will see a drastic increase not just in the number of customers you get, but also their value. Customers who come in through content marketing will be eager to use your product, because they already know and trust you. If your experience is the same as that of the companies mentioned in this book, these customers are more likely to spend more money with you, are more likely to remain customers, and are more likely to refer others to your business.

PROCEED WITH CAUTION: DELIVERING VALUE BY ENTERTAINING

In addition to solving customers' problems, you can also deliver value by providing entertainment. The big caveat with this strategy for delivering value is that most people are not as funny as they think. *More often than not, being funny fails.* However, if you are, in fact, very funny, clever, and entertaining, or if you can hire someone who is, entertainment is a great way to deliver value to people.

The Old Spice guy is a great example of this. He's funny and entertaining, and that's valuable to people. The Old Spice strategy worked especially well, because deodorant is a low-cognition product. You're not going to spend three-and-a-half hours researching which deodorant to buy. You're just at Target in the deodorant aisle and looking at all your choices when your eyes land on Old Spice. The memory of the commercial pops up in your head, so that's the deodorant you throw into your basket. It's a recognizable and familiar name. It stuck with you, because the Old Spice guy is hilarious.

This strategy can work for higher-end products, too. Blendtec blenders are pricey and high-powered. The company put out a YouTube series a few years ago called, "Will It Blend?" This series is exactly what it sounds like: they try to blend everything from food to an iPad to a phonebook to binoculars. There's something ridiculous, funny, and memorable about watching an iPad go through a blender. Also, it's the sort of thing that a viewer is likely to pass along to a friend. This was a win for Blendtec and made people more willing to fork over several hundred dollars for their product the next time they found themselves in need of a blender.

DIFFERENTIATING YOURSELF FROM THE PACK

If you're thinking, "Well, all of this sounds pretty simple," that's because it is. Yet these simple things can get you far ahead of your competition, because most people just don't think in these terms. Most marketers love trying to figure out the best "growth hack" or the "hidden strategy" to set them apart from everyone else. They latch on to the hottest trends. But the truth is, the simplest strategies are often the most effective. Johnson & Johnson knew that in 1888, and savvy marketers still know it today.

Every day, it gets a bit more difficult to differentiate ourselves from the pack, because the barrier to entry for starting a business is increasingly lower and lower. Once upon a time, just *being* in business was enough to get people's attention. Additionally, it's becoming easier and easier to copy other businesses' software or hardware—hello, 3D printing—because, again, the cost of doing so is lower than it has ever been. If you create a product that shows signs of success, then the question isn't *if* someone else is going to copy it; the question is *when* it will be copied. The next question is: will that competitor be able to out-market you? This trend isn't going away. It's only going to get easier to build software and hardware, which means your product isn't enough to set you apart from everyone else's anymore. Not if you want to build a profitable and, just as important, *sustainable* business.

It's those things that *aren't* commodities that have kept a lot of modern companies alive and thriving—things such as trust, authority, and a real relationship with their audience. These assets act as insurance against the threats of commoditization. If you have a software product, and you have built deep relationships with your customers and prospects, it becomes much more difficult for competitors to copy you. In fact, trust and authority *can't* be copied. So, if another company enters the market with the same product as yours, but you have already established trust and authority, then your audience is likely to stay put. *This* is why content marketing is more important than ever. For most businesses, it's the easiest and most reliable method for establishing all the intangible assets that will secure your business for the long haul.

DON'T JUST DO IT: DO IT *WELL*

For content marketing to succeed, it has to be done well. Part of the reason content marketing has received a bad rap is because *anyone* can do it. It costs almost nothing in terms of money or time to start a WordPress site or Medium account, write a few articles and hit Publish. "There!" our would-be marketer thinks, "I'm doing content marketing." Ten times out of ten, that approach doesn't work, and the marketer is left shrugging their shoulders, saying, "I tried content marketing. It didn't work."

Content marketing definitively *does* work, but, as case after case demonstrates, it only works when it's done right. It works when you invest time and resources into doing an extraordinarily good job of building incredibly valuable content. When you do that, and then promote your content intelligently and strategically, content marketing absolutely works.

There's a big difference between now and fifteen years ago, when companies like HubSpot paved the way for digital content marketing. At that point, a company that did pretty much *any* type of content marketing would see results, simply because no one else was doing it. It was such a novel idea that it was interesting and unique to audiences, which meant companies could win with little effort. This success brought a lot of attention to content marketing, which soon gave way to content farms: outsourced agencies that sell content—really, really bad content—by the pound. Now *that's* a good way to check content marketing off your to-do list, right?

Wrong. Effective content marketing requires much more than just getting someone to write content for you. It requires deeply understanding your audience and using that understanding as the foundation to publish content that's useful, interesting, and unique. That doesn't come at two cents per word. Content farms are a very enticing option when you're a marketing executive with dozens of marketing channels under your purview, and you simply have no time to research or thoughtfully craft content.

More than ever, people can smell bad content marketing from a mile away, because we've all seen so much of it. It comes in the form of bland content that's neither useful nor interesting. Now, because of all this clutter, it takes more to get people's attention. To win at content marketing, you have to devote real attention and energy to creating content that's extraordinary.

CONTENT COMES BEFORE CHANNEL

Notice that with all this talk about content, I have largely steered clear of specific words like *blog*, *video*, or *infographic*. Great content will be successful on just about any channel—whether it's Facebook, YouTube, LinkedIn, Pinterest, or anything else—if your customers are active on that channel. In fact, the same great content can exist on many channels.

With this in mind, I encourage you to start, not by thinking about the channel, but about the content itself. If you get too attached to creating a podcast or blogging or producing a video, you risk missing the mark. By thinking about the channel first, you are assuming that your audience's focus is on that channel, and that it's the most high-leverage way to get their attention. This is an incorrect, baseless assumption.

Let's say you're an executive at a consulting company, and you spend a lot of your time on LinkedIn. It makes sense based on your own experience, LinkedIn comes to mind when you think about what channel your company should be investing in. However, your audience may not consist mainly of executives, and they might not care about LinkedIn that much. The inverse is also often true. Many business owners assume that some channels are wrong for their audience, simply because the business owners themselves aren't on them. "I don't think doctors are on Instagram," a medical software marketer might say. Based on Instagram's *actual* user data, that marketer is wrong.

WHAT ABOUT TRENDS?

If everyone else is making listicles, shouldn't you jump on that train? Not necessarily. Trends are important to mass-market-media publishers, but quality is not a trend. Quality is not going away, either.

Remember that the definition of *good* content marketing changes often, which is yet another reason not to get too caught up in any one method. Six months from now, the "best" method will be different from what it is today. Betty Crocker is one of my favorite examples in terms of how medium and method change over time. In the 1950s, long before the phrase "content marketing" existed, Betty Crocker was doing exactly that by publishing recipes on the back of General Mills packaging. The suburban mom who was looking at the packages wasn't thinking, "Oh, content marketing!" She was looking at her cake mix box and thinking, "Oh, that's valuable! Before I throw this box away, I'm going to cut this recipe out and save it."

Unlike all the other packaging that people threw out, Betty Crocker's was so valuable that people would store it in their kitchen drawers. In some cases, they even passed this marketing-in-the-form-of-recipes down through the generations.

Amazing content marketing shouldn't feel like marketing at all. It's just going to feel like value. You should be thinking about every piece the same way—you want it to be too valuable to throw out. If somebody bookmarks it, e-mails it to themselves, or pins it, you know you've hit on incredibly valuable content marketing.

YOU'RE COMPETING WITH SOCIAL MEDIA

One final reason for only publishing extraordinary content: if you do anything at all on the Internet, you're competing with social media. On average, people spend 116 minutes per day, or a total of five years of their life on social media. When you're trying to get people's attention on the Internet, you're competing with Facebook, Twitter, Pinterest, and Instagram. Not only that, but you're also competing with their work, their phone, and the errands they have to run. Just getting someone to click on your content requires a pretty good sale. What if they do all that work, forsaking every other distraction on the Internet to get to your site, and you let them down? They're not coming back.

Don't let this stop you. There *is* a margin for error, in the sense that you can and *should* play with your content-marketing tactics. Test things. Try different approaches. Take a controversial position. Try a completely "off-brand" voice. See what happens! You shouldn't be afraid of making a blunder: you probably won't break much. No matter what you do or test, your goal should always be to make whatever you publish the absolute best of its kind on the Internet. Anything less will be ignored.

ONE MORE STORY

Before we get into the nitty-gritty of all this, I want to leave you with one last story.

Once upon a time, it was difficult to sell tires, because cars weren't prevalent yet, and people weren't driving everywhere. Michelin, the now-famous tire company, realized that sending out tire catalogs was a bad sales tactic, because no one really cared. They also realized if they could just find a way to get people to drive more, these drivers would need new tires at some point. Their answer? *Michelin Guides.* They published guides pointing people to great restaurants, hotels, and landmarks throughout France—and later, the rest of Europe and beyond. Places that people would have to *drive* to. Sure enough, since people were driving more, they needed more tires. Michelin Guides became a household name and Michelin tires took off. Another example of a company providing value and, thus, establishing trust with its audience.

CHAPTER TWO

FIND OUT WHAT YOUR CUSTOMERS REALLY WANT

One of the most common mistakes companies make is basing their content-marketing campaigns on assumptions. These assumptions are generally about what their customers want to read or *don't* want to read. By doing this, content creators inadvertently create content that reflects their own assumptions, rather than speaking to their audience's true pain points.

These assumptions are perilous. You can write the best content in the world, but if you're writing it without the right people in mind, then the chances of it connecting with your audience are slim. Finding this connection is key; if your content isn't achieving this, your efforts are useless.

THE CURSE OF THE EXPERT

Another common pitfall when creating content is presuming everyone else knows as much as you do. Some call this "the curse of the expert." In many cases, the person or people in charge of content have years of experience in their particular industry. After even just a couple of years in an industry, we take for granted all the knowledge we've acquired. Sure, other people within the industry may know more than we do, but the average person on the outside, including your audience, probably does not.

Too often, marketers write content that's *too* advanced for their customers. As you'll see when you go through some of the customer-interview exercises in the next chapter, chances are your customers' problems are far more basic than you think. But to you, addressing these basic issues and challenges might feel as if the information you're providing your customers isn't at all substantive. You think your content is far too simple to be useful to anyone.

It's okay to feel like this, but it's also important to understand that most of your customers' deepest pain will seem simple to you. Very rarely will you find your audience is dealing with highly technical or sophisticated challenges. For example, if you sell kitchen appliances, you may assume your customers are especially concerned with technical aspects of appliance shopping, such as why BTUs per square inch is a better measure of a good stove than total BTUs. You know, the things that are interesting *to* you. However, *what your customers really want are simple tips for making a stressful choice easier.* Something along the lines of: "I need a new stove and I don't even know where to start." The information may seem overly simplistic as far as you're concerned, but it's this sort of thing that keeps your customers awake at night. The thorns in our sides, the things we want answers for, are often basic things.

Understanding this is half of the battle. Across the board, you'll find that creating content about these fundamental topics is going to connect with people more than the highly technical concepts you're an expert in, even if that seems unbelievable from where you're standing.

I was working with a Fortune 500 financial services company to build a content hub that would house more than 300 pieces of content. The content they had been publishing up to that point was quite sophisticated. It wasn't rocket-science complicated, but it went beyond the basics of explaining the difference between a traditional, Roth, and 401(k) IRA. Instead, this company's existing content delved into subjects like tax codes and other topics over their average reader's head. The marketing team's logic was that this sophisticated content would be unique and set them apart from competitors. They assumed their audience was eager to learn the ins and outs of personal finance and investment vehicles. I appreciated their enthusiasm, but let me ask: have *you* Googled "investment vehicles" lately?

This company provides retirement accounts and insurance to employees of other large firms. Their customers are regular Americans who have no desire to learn about the detailed back stories of various investment vehicles.

I assumed we were missing the mark, but I wanted to be sure. Upon surveying more than 200 of the company's customers, we confirmed that, indeed, they had no interest in investment vehicles. They wanted to know the basics, like: How does a checking account differ from a savings account? What do I need to know when I'm buying a house? How do I save on groceries?

We built an array of content to address the challenges we uncovered, but the team was afraid to publish it. They were worried they would look foolish by publishing obvious information that would bore their audience to tears or, worse, seem condescending. This feedback came from people who spent many years on Wall Street, so the content was all second nature to them. The point is that it's *not* second nature to most people, including their audience.

Sure enough, when we published the content, it was the pieces the team deemed simplistic that ended up being the most effective. Analytics showed us that their audience engaged the most with content that focused on effectively breaking down the basics.

USEFUL IS VALUABLE

We human beings want to look smart. It's a status thing. We expect that others will have more respect for us if we are. This translates to assuming that our customers are more likely to buy from us if they know we're intelligent. The problem is that sometimes this desire to look smart conflicts with our ability to be useful.

Useful is more valuable than smart, and it takes a lot of intelligence to take a complex topic and distill it to the point where anyone can understand it.

I did a consulting project for a firm that specializes in tax accounting for start-ups. One of the things I heard over and over from their customers was they struggled with their bookkeeping. Their customers' questions seemed simple to the accountants. What percent of my income should I be putting away for taxes? What are estimated taxes? How does getting married impact my taxes? These accountants, who spent their days buried in spreadsheets and engaged in abstract arguments with the IRS about the nuances of the tax code, couldn't believe that *this* is what their clients wanted to learn about.

We responded to the firm's audience's needs with a video Q&A series. A lot of the questions we answered were sourced from our initial customer interviews. Right away, their customers loved this series, and they began to share it with their friends and colleagues. The content quickly spread, and viewers wrote in with even more basic questions for the accountants to answer.

It was humbling for the accountants to see how valuable the basics were to their customers. They realized it wasn't their knowledge of obscure tax codes that won people over, but being useful in a way that people could understand.

We did publish one advanced Q&A topic for the accounting firm as a bit of an experiment. Nothing. The audience simply didn't care.

Don't worry about explaining all the advanced, obscure things you know to your customers. Just help people trust that you know more about the topic than they do. The simplest and most effective route to accomplish this is by explaining concepts that seem basic to you in a way that also makes them basic to everybody else. If you can do this from a unique perspective—more on that later—then you'll win.

IMPOSTER'S SYNDROME

There is a flip side to the curse of the expert, which is Imposter's Syndrome. Those suffering from Imposter's Syndrome don't view themselves as experts. In their mind, plenty of people are far more qualified, more credentialed, and more experienced than they are on a given topic. So, why should anybody listen to little ol' them?

Although this manifests in the opposite problem, it comes back to the same point as the Curse of the Expert, which is that there's tremendous value in solving basic problems for people. Here's the thing: If you spend a few hours really digging into online research, diving deep into a particular topic, you'll become an expert relative to almost everybody—certainly, relative to 99 percent of those who comprise your market. Just by going out, doing the research, and curating an answer and a solution, you're creating great value, because that's a few hours work your audience doesn't have to do.

I'm not an expert on buying homeowner's insurance, but I'm confident that with a few hours of focused research, I could learn more about the topic than the majority of first-time buyers know. With a bit more work, I could research and create content that would usefully answer many of the burning questions facing those first-time buyers.

Your team's lack of expertise can even be an asset. In Groove's case, the fact that we were experiencing many of these challenges for the first time—and publishing about how we tackled them—became a compelling story for our readers who wanted to follow along and learn with us.

Also, credentialed "experts" may be viewed as intimidating and untouchable by regular people who are seeking basic information. Let's say I want to learn about string theory, for example. Am I going to seek out the most published and decorated researcher on string theory and read her most influential research papers? *No!* I'm going to surf on over to the string theory Wikipedia page, which will explain the concept in an efficient and basic way I can wrap my head around. That's all I need to know.

TALKING TO YOUR CUSTOMERS

The first follow-up meeting I have with a company after interviewing their customers is always interesting. On one hand, we now have a mountain of rich, thorough insights from customers about their challenges, pain, struggles, and desires, as well as what specifically will make them happy. On the other hand, there is the content the company has been publishing so far. The gap between these two is usually incredible, not only in terms of topics but language. So often, they're just downright misaligned.

Without the alignment of topic, tone, voice, and language, it's almost impossible to connect with your audience. The good news is that bridging this gap isn't complicated. All it really involves is simple research or, more specifically, talking to your customers.

These conversations don't happen as a matter of course for many reasons, one of which is that marketers don't get promoted—at least, not directly—for talking to customers. It's not unusual for a company's content creator—let's call her Amy—to have never spoken with a customer during her tenure at the firm. Amy was hired as a content writer, and unless her boss really understands content marketing, she was probably hired because Amy's boss expects her to know exactly what to say. After all, Amy is a great writer, right?

Part of an effective content writer's job must be to gain a deep understanding of the language customers use. Most companies miss this step altogether. If you can familiarize yourself with the exact words people use to discuss their problems—which we'll talk about shortly—and specifically address an issue they've been struggling with for months or years, your content becomes downright irresistible. In some cases, you might even be able to articulate issues your audience hasn't been able to find the right words for yet. It's like you took the words right out of their mouths!

Unfortunately, most companies who create marketing content have never experienced this magic, because they've skipped over the practice of talking to their customers. This happens for a few main reasons. Perhaps they're scared to do it, feel like they're too busy, or don't want to do it. None of these reasons is good enough to justify skipping this critical step.

We have these built-in assumptions about our customers' desires, dreams, fears, and goals. We don't live in a culture that loves challenging assumptions, so, for most of us, it doesn't feel natural to go out and do something that might change what we think. We're scared of being wrong. These discussions can be uncomfortable.

However, the beauty of doing anything uncomfortable is that it sets you apart. Most companies won't do things outside their comfort zones. This means if you are willing to live with a bit of discomfort, you're already way ahead of the masses—and probably your competition.

DON'T PUT WORDS IN YOUR CUSTOMERS' MOUTHS

Another reason why these conversations with customers are so important is because they breach the often-massive divide between our audiences' description of an issue and our interpretation of it. Anything we see, learn, or capture is filtered through our own lens. This lens is colored by our experiences in life and our field, our knowledge, and our expertise. A customer might say, "I want X," but we hear, "X isn't your product, but I want your product, so I want you to add this feature to your product." Notice that that is not what the customer said. At all.

There is no substitute for the actual words your customers use to describe their experiences, desires, and challenges.

In the absence of a conversation, we are providing words and sentiments for our customers to respond to. The minute you reword or revise their statements to sound nice, feel more *sales-y* or *marketing-y*, or reframe them through your own perspective, you've lost any chance of creating the deep connection that speaking at your customers' level will breed.

FACILITATING AN OPEN-ENDED CONVERSATION

Now that we've established the need to talk to your customers, let's talk about *how* to do it. This strategy is of particular importance to those who tend to be quantitatively minded. They think in terms of how many survey responses are necessary for statistical significance. My advice: don't worry about it.

We're not going for statistical significance, because statistical significance means we're trying to get a mathematically defensible sense of averages or most common responses. What we want for our purpose is *practical* significance. We want to get people who are going to delve deeply into particular pain or pleasure points, or hopes, fears, and dreams. That's where emotion lives, and that's what we're interested in. If you have a few customers discussing the same thing in depth, you'll glean information about a topic that a lot of your customers really care about, as opposed to plotting data points on a map. Data points do little to convey customer language or translate emotion.

Most companies can achieve a good sampling of the information they need from their customers by talking to just a handful of people. If you have thousands of customers, talk to thirty or forty. If you have hundreds of customers, talk to ten. If you have dozens of customers, talk to a few. And if you have just a few customers, talk to all of them. Ask them open-ended questions over the phone or in person. Get them talking. If you stumble onto something they actually care about, they'll talk for a long, long time. That's where you'll find the language, emotion, and intonation you need to make great content.

Open-ended questions give your customers the chance to direct the conversation. A multiple-choice question, which is, by definition, a closed question, such as, "What is your greatest interior decorating challenge?" eliminates any chance of hearing your customer's language. It also leads customers to respond based on the assumption that one of five possible answers captures his or her thoughts and opinions, which may very well not be the case. What if their greatest interior decorating challenge isn't one of the choices?

Even an open-ended question can be leading. If you lead your audience, you are naturally going to get the answers you expect. This affirms that your assumption was "correct," regardless of what the case may be. You've gained nothing.

Let's say I'm working for a company that develops customer service software. A bad open-ended question might be something like, "What customer service software are you currently using?" As innocuous and non-leading as this question may seem at first glance, it presupposes the person actually *uses* customer service software. This is a big and often false assumption.

An effective open-ended alternative would be, "How are you answering customer service e-mails now?" or "What do you wish was different about your customer service workflow?" This question would alert me to the fact that 10 to 20 percent of the market isn't currently using customer support software, nor do they have any intention of incorporating it into their business. I might learn they're using a shared inbox of some sort instead, which is extremely valuable information for me to have.

SIX QUESTIONS THAT WILL LEAD YOU TO THE ANSWERS YOU NEED

Creating open-ended questions may sound easy, but it can be difficult to strike the right balance between not leading respondents, while still giving them enough specificity that their answers will be useful to you. Use these tested questions to evoke illuminating answers that will help you help your audience.

1. *Tell me about your experience with [insert your product].*

With this opening question, you direct the conversation, while still keeping it specific enough that the respondent's answers are relevant.

2. *What's your biggest challenge with X?*

This narrows the funnel a bit. Also, the word "challenge" is important, because it's not a negative word. Negative words—like "problem"—can lead respondents to discuss troubles that aren't pertinent, because that's what you're asking for.

3. *How are you currently dealing with these challenges?*

This question will let you know what you're up against, whether it's a competing product or just apathy.

4. *What have you tried to solve these challenges that didn't work?*

Knowing which approaches your audience has abandoned and why will help you tackle one of the biggest objections you'll face: "Well, I already tried X, and it didn't work."

5. What would solving these challenges allow you to achieve?

This will tell you why solving this problem is important to your audience, which is invaluable for framing your content. The whole point of solving people's problems is to help them achieve a specific goal. If you can talk about that goal in the same way they see it, you will do a much better job of convincing them to read about your solution.

6. What blogs do you read frequently? What online communities are you a part of?

Understanding who your audiences' influencers are will help you study the content that resonates with them. It will also help you later on when it's time to promote your content. (Much more on this in Chapter 5.)

I'll leave you with one final anecdote about why the phrasing of questions is so important in obtaining meaningful answers. My friend Noah Kagan was the first marketer at Mint, a personal finance tracking app that launched in 2006. Before they launched, the Mint team spent weeks surveying their target market to figure out what it really wanted.

Take a moment here and rewind to 2006. If you were to guess, who do you think Mint found their biggest competitor to be? If you thought of a company like Intuit or MS

Money, you made a smart guess. However, you're wrong. Through their research, Mint came to find out that the number one company they were competing against was… *no one*. It turned out that Mint's target audience would rather not track *anything* and just see their balance when they went to the ATM.

Think about how profoundly that changed Mint's message. Now, rather than convincing people that Mint was better than every other piece of personal finance software out there, Mint had to convince their audience that this is a problem they should solve with software, *period*. The answers Mint heard were extremely helpful, and they were able to obtain them with smart, thorough surveys.

KEEP THE CONVERSATION GOING

Good marketers start by talking to their customers. Great marketers never stop. They regularly check in to see how needs and interests are changing. I don't want to scare you into thinking that talking to customers is all you'll do now, but I do want you to realize this also isn't a one-and-done process. Plan to speak to a sampling of your customer base quarterly and certainly no less than twice a year. This doesn't mean you have to constantly sample large groups, but it is important to touch base with a handful of customers a few times a year to get a gauge on whether or not anything has changed, and if so, what. Just a few fifteen- to thirty-minute conversations will give you an advantage over most competitors.

People change, markets change, desires change, channels change, and trends change. External factors influence every market. Everybody is going to conferences, meeting with people, and hearing about the next big thing. It used to be really cool, sexy, and cutting-edge to have a mobile-friendly website. Now customers expect it. Outdated customer insights don't help you and in fact might even hurt you by making you appear out of step.

In most quarters, your check-in conversations with customers will serve as an affirmation that your insights still hold up, with perhaps a few slight changes. But there will come a quarter when a couple of responses start to veer in a slightly new direction. You will become aware of rumblings of new ideas, different challenges, and factors that didn't previously exist.

Going back to the customer service software example, there might be several quarters when everything stays the same. Then, during a quarterly check-in, one customer asks, "What about live chat? Shouldn't we be doing live chat on our site?" Then the next quarter, two customers ask this question. The following quarter, four customers ask. You've now spotted a trend. When you query the larger market about this topic, you find that 18 percent of your audience now considers live chat important. You now have something to focus on and can change your strategy accordingly.

ENTERING NEW MARKETS

Even if you don't yet have customers, chances are you know who you're trying to target. These are the people you want to talk to. One of the ways to find these folks is to go where they hang out online. If you're seeking out realtors, they might gravitate to very specific real estate forums, blogs, or websites. If, on the other hand, you're selling real estate, your audience is probably a little more dispersed. There's not a single online community where everybody is buying houses, so they're probably spread across different sites like City-Data.com and various local communities, forums, and e-mail lists.

Find those people. See what they're writing about and what they're struggling with. Then take those responses and turn them into content. Take the *exact* language people are using on these outlets to describe their challenges and solve that problem through your content.

I also find review sites to be helpful. Books and articles have already been written about almost every conceivable problem. Go to Amazon and search for books that solve the same problems you want to address. I followed this exact strategy for a tax accounting company that came to me for help putting together materials for a trade show they were slated to attend the following week. Because of the tight timeline, we didn't have time to survey a group of customers. Instead, we went on Amazon and researched books about tax accounting for small businesses. We looked at the four- and five-star reviews to figure out what people loved about these books. Within these reviews, we looked for language in much the same way we would have in a phone call with a customer. Where did the tone of the review get impassioned? What do these people care about a lot?

People really loved the top-performing books because they simplified basic principles. We saw that customers appreciated it when books explained exactly what to do to achieve certain results without necessitating a lot of expenditure on other resources. Many readers specifically loved being given a simple way to understand which receipts and records needed to be saved, and which could be discarded. This fueled some of the highest-performing content pieces we created on this project.

Next, we looked at one- and two-star reviews. What did people find lacking in these books? What were they missing? Where did they drop the ball? Again, we learned a lot about what people wanted but couldn't find. We based our content on this gap. It worked! Not only was the trade show a success for the firm, but they were able to use the content to appeal to new customers for years to come.

This process is so simple that people overlook it. It's incredible how much information you can glean from review sites like Yelp and TripAdvisor, or whichever platforms apply specifically to your field. Find out what people love and hate about your competitors. Learn what they struggle with and use that to feed your content. You can position your entire marketing strategy around research that's right at your fingertips.

CHAPTER THREE

CREATE CONTENT THAT CONNECTS

Once you get to the root of your customers' pain points and know what their deepest challenges are, the next step is to help them solve those problems. Figuring this out can be intimidating, but there are several different ways to do so effectively.

Your biggest advantage is just how *little* time and research most people put into solving their problems. They put in a lot of emotion and energy into *suffering* from their problems, but very little into *solving* them.

It reminds me of how my wife and I used to keep a paper grocery bag on our kitchen floor, where we would put our recycling. Both of us would cringe every time we saw this bag because it looked ugly, but we never did anything about it. In fact, we used an old grocery bag for *years* until we finally spent the hour it took to buy a decorative basket that now houses our recycling bag. I had every opportunity to solve that problem for years, but I didn't; I just thought about it. The same is true of most problems that people, including your customers, face.

With just a few hours of online research, you will know more about how to solve your customers' problems than they do, simply because you put in the time.

This doesn't mean you should pretend to be an expert when you're not. If it makes you more comfortable, feel free to be honest about the fact that you lack experience in a particular area, and simply share the process you're using to solve the problem yourself. We took this approach at Groove, where our start-up-focused content proudly said, "Hey, we don't know the solution, but we're going to figure it out, and you'll probably find value in coming along for the ride."

THE LANGUAGE CONNECTION

The words you choose play a critical role in creating a connection with your audience. As we discussed in the previous chapter, not only do you want to understand your customers' problems, you also want to understand *how they talk about these problems*. Because unless you speak the same language as your customers, you'll never be able to convince them that you understand them.

If you're not writing like your customer, you're probably

writing in marketing- or business-speak. This is, after all, what we're taught to do as marketers, entrepreneurs, and business leaders. It's "professional." In reality, this professional jargon is the worst way to write.

How often do you turn to a friend and say, "Gee, I really wish there were a more robust app for this?" If you're like most people, the answer is "never." People don't talk this way. But some app makers still use words like "robust" to promote their products to audiences that don't care.

Smart people—like your audience—can smell marketing from miles away. They're surrounded by it in their inbox, newsfeed, and everywhere else they look. They've developed an immunity to it. When your marketing smells like marketing, it's impossible to get your audience to let their guard down and allow a connection to happen.

If you make just one change to your content-marketing program, I encourage you to start mirroring your customers' language. It will change your results dramatically for the better.

CUTTING THROUGH CORPORATE-SPEAK

Using your customers' language sometimes becomes a bit more challenging when you're marketing for a larger company. This doesn't mean it's not possible for larger corporations to speak their customers' language, or even that the process is any less straightforward. The issue is red tape. Many larger companies have established brand guidelines that include parameters for tone and ways of speaking. These guidelines are typically owned by a branding or marketing department tasked with making sure that all outgoing collateral and messaging is "on brand."

Although being *on brand* isn't a bad thing, it can be prohibitive for content marketing, since these guidelines are traditionally designed for advertising. Remember, content marketing is about much more than just making a sale; it's about building a relationship over a long period of time. But brand guidelines, by definition, are designed to make you sound like a brand. It's very hard to hold someone's attention, engagement, and trust over a long period of time when this is the case. Very few of us identify as being "in a relationship" with a brand. Do you remember the last time you thought, "Man, I feel like this brand understands me!" Building that relationship requires a human touch.

This conflict is exacerbated in larger companies, because copy is often required to go through a compliance department or legal review. Those who perform such reviews are tasked with stripping away any content that runs the risk of being offensive or creating liability. When unchecked, this can lead to content that's broad, generic, boring, and, frankly, valueless. Compliance departments have good reasons for performing these checks and balances; it's just that their systems and regulations don't always work to the benefit of content marketing.

Smaller companies don't have to contend with this sort of logistical red tape. Typically, the content team or creator is empowered to publish content, and that's the end of it. More than likely, there will be some pushback if this sort of system is proposed at a larger company. The process of getting through that pushback is often uncomfortable, but can be worth it.

The first work-around is to hire an outside content firm that won't be afraid to challenge your company's processes. I worked with a Fortune 500 financial company on several hundred pieces of content designed to help people wrap their head around finance, save money, and make savvier investment decisions. We were working with a new digital department that was really excited about what we'd put together. It was fresh and different from the company's past content efforts, and we were confident it would speak to the firm's clients in a way that none of their existing content did. When the time came to publish the content, though, I was stopped in my tracks. "Okay, we just have to send it through compliance first." I could hear the record scratch to a halt.

First of all, I was told it would take between two and three months for this content to make its way through compliance. Second, I knew from experience that when it was returned to us, the amount of red ink would be blinding. The "safe" version of our content would have all its personality and resonance stripped away.

"Hey," I said. "I understand this is the process, but what if we *don't* put this content through compliance? What if we just publish it?" My contact got visibly uncomfortable. "What do you mean?" he asked. "We can't do that! I could lose my job." I don't want a friend of mine or anyone else to risk their job, but *I* didn't work for the company, right?

"Listen," I told him, "I have access to your website. I can upload the content. What if I just put it up there? We could get it in front of people quickly to see the impact."

And, so, after assuring my contact that I would take full responsibility, that's exactly what I did. For several years now, this content has been live on the company's site, and compliance hasn't said a word. Meanwhile, the campaign has performed extremely well for the company. So well, in fact, that they've since dedicated an entire team to working on it full-time.

I am not advocating that you put your job on the line. What you *can* do, however, is plant a small seed by skirting the rules a bit. Start with a small project you can safely ask forgiveness rather than permission for. You don't even have to publish it if you don't feel comfortable doing so. Just create great content, ask a few customers for their feedback, and then review the results. Once you see that not only does your content work, but your audience actually *loves it*, it will become easier to make the decision to just hit "publish."

Your content has to be good for this strategy to work. It's critical to understand that this is a key element to your success. Creating good content isn't an easy thing to do, but it *is* straightforward if you follow all the guidelines established in this book. If you're guided by the intention of solving people's problems and being useful, interesting, and unique, you'll end up with good content.

People will forgive prose that isn't flowery and poetic. People will forgive design that isn't polished and gorgeous. People will forgive production quality that isn't world-class. People will forgive all these things as long as the substance of the content delivers value.

> **THE BENEFITS OF BEING LARGE**
>
> This seems like a good opportunity to point out that while larger companies may present some additional hurdles to overcome, these are counterbalanced by certain benefits that smaller companies don't have access to.
>
> One of the most challenging elements of building an effective content marketing program is getting your target audience to see it. Most large companies already have a big audience. They already have established website traffic and e-mail subscribers. They have a captive audience.
>
> Not only this, but large companies also have more resources to facilitate conversations with customers and can develop and produce great content.

THE GOOD CONTENT TRIFECTA

Good content should have three primary qualities: it should be useful, interesting, and unique. Useful means that its audience sees the content as having value and being actionable. Interesting means that it makes people want to read it. Unique means that even if you're talking about topics that have been discussed before, you're doing so with a perspective or angle that hasn't been widely used.

All too often, companies try to emulate the dominant players in the content-marketing field. This *especially* happens when it comes to writing about content marketing itself. HubSpot, a content-marketing company, was one of the big players early on in digital content. Others saw the success of HubSpot and figured they would follow its proven formula.

For a while there, the market was flooded with content that closely mimicked HubSpot's strategy, framing, voice, tone, and language. On paper, this makes sense, but here's the problem: No one else was going to be a better HubSpot than HubSpot. Just like no one else is going to be a better Geico than Geico, or a better Groove than Groove. If you want to win, you have to be the very best version of yourself you possibly can. You have to offer unique value. There has to be something about your content that makes your customer want to listen to you despite all the other things that are competing for their attention.

This doesn't mean that any topic your competitors are already publishing content about is off-limits, which is a good thing, because there's virtually no problem under the sun that hasn't already been written about in books, blogs, or articles. Consider personal finance, for example. People have been struggling with personal finance for hundreds of years, but still, every year, there's a new bestseller in the personal finance category. Likewise, people have been grappling with productivity forever. Every year, like clockwork, there's a new bestseller in the productivity category. Same thing with health, parenting, gardening, and anything else that people struggle with. You can absolutely talk about things other people have already talked about; you just have to do it from a unique perspective.

CHAPTER FOUR

GET YOUR MESSAGE TO YOUR MARKET

Once your content is ready to publish, your next job is to get it in front of your target audience. As we've already discussed, like anything else in business, content marketing is not just a matter of building something; it's also about getting people to act on it.

THE POWER OF INFLUENCE

There are dozens of different strategies for accomplishing this. A lot of people use paid advertising. I've found influencer marketing, also known as content promotion, to be more effective and certainly more cost-effective. The idea behind it is this: You may not yet have a big audience hanging on your every word. You might not have a long list of e-mail addresses to send to or social media followers who are anxiously awaiting your next post. But other people *do* have this sort of reach in your market. And if you can get these influencers on your side, you, too, can have their reach.

These influencers have spent years building trust, authority, and relationships with a large audience. These trendsetters exist somewhere in your market because, at this point, they exist in almost *every* market. It's these influencers your prospective customers and readers are paying attention to. That's why getting their help is so valuable.

Before we dive into the details of how to do this, there is one important caveat: as is the case with any strategy that works, businesses have sprung up around the concept of influencer marketing in order to profit off the idea. If you Google "influencer marketing," you will find services that claim they can act as the middle man, essentially brokering influencers to promote your content. *This does not work most of the time.* These services will generally just spam an influencer list they purchased with a message that says no more than, "Hey, will you please share this post on Twitter?" It amounts to junk and is far more hurtful than helpful. Much as spamming your market with bad content doesn't work, neither does spamming influencers.

BUILDING RELATIONSHIPS WITH INFLUENCERS

If you are still in the process of building your own following, it is more efficient to build relationships with influencers than it is to build an audience of readers one-by-one. The key phrase here is "build relationships." Many people err by doing what mass influence marketers do—sending out a template e-mail to hundreds of influencers asking them to share a piece of content.

This tactic is about as effective as a Nigerian prince e-mail scam, and even more dangerous to your reputation. These influencers have put a lot of time and effort into building a trusting relationship with their audience. Why on earth would they risk giving someone they don't know access to that audience?

These influencers are gatekeepers, and the way through the gate—and to your audience—is by building a relationship with them. This requires the same things of you that great content marketing does. It requires you to provide value and solve problems. Only now, you're doing this for influencers rather than your end audience. Sure, these influencers may not have the same problems as your audience, but they, like everyone else on this planet, absolutely have problems for which they want solutions. If you can provide these solutions by thinking creatively, the keys to the kingdom will be yours.

IDENTIFYING INFLUENCERS

If you're not already aware of who the big movers and shakers are in your market, there are a few ways to find them. First, remember your existing customers are a huge asset. When you speak with them, ask a few targeted questions that will lead you straight to influencers. Questions like: What sites or blogs do you read every day? Where do you spend most of your time online? What forums do you visit? It's easy to work these questions into both your content marketing and the other one-off conversations you might find yourself having with customers.

This is another place your knowledge of customers' problems can pay off. Once you understand the issues that are plaguing your audience, you can dig around to determine who is already working to solve them. Who has blogs, social media, and YouTube channels focused on these issues? Check industry forums to see whose articles on the topic are being shared, or if there are influencers who are contributing to those forums. You can also search the Internet to find the most popular pieces of content about the issue.

A site called BuzzSumo is also a great resource for identifying influencers. To use it, simply enter the URL of an article that addresses a topic relevant to your market. BuzzSumo will then generate a list of all the people who publicly shared that article. You might, for example, check to see how many Twitter followers a sharer has. Not only is this easy, but it's also valuable for uncovering the people you may be unaware of who have a solid following and are interested in the type of content you're publishing.

Go the Extra Mile

In this day and age, when everyone is trying to connect with influencers online, you can set yourself apart by making a face-to-face connection with an influencer. Remember, the key here is building relationships by delivering value.

Early on in my career, I lived in Washington, DC, and wanted to meet a well-known marketer in Los Angeles so I could get advice. I put in quite a bit of time online trying to spark this relationship by thoughtfully commenting on his articles. This led to an e-mail relationship, and I would periodically send him links I thought he might find interesting. When I met another well-known marketer in New York City whom I thought my Los Angeles contact would enjoy meeting, I offered to introduce them, because I believed the meeting could be mutually beneficial. Sure enough, they were excited about the connection and hit it off.

After about a year of nurturing this relationship, I asked if we could set aside fifteen minutes to meet when I visited LA for a meeting later that month. He responded that he would be out of town on those dates, but to let him know the next time I found myself in LA. A couple of days later, I told him my meeting was rescheduled. Could he meet the following week instead? "Absolutely," he responded. "Let's make it happen."

There was no other meeting in Los Angeles. I took a gamble that this relationship would be worth the investment. It turns out it was. Many years later, he's still a mentor and has helped tremendously in my career. I'm certain that our relationship is so solid because I went out of my way to make an in-person connection. (For the record, yes, I later told him about my harebrained scheme, which he found hilarious.)

There really is no amount of e-mailing or commenting that can equal half an hour of face-time with someone. Few people are willing to do that extra bit of work or spend the extra time and resources it takes. It's worth it. The end result is getting to play on a completely different level than everyone else in your industry. It's how you not only come to know the influencers in your field, but ultimately evolve into one yourself.

REACHING OUT TO INFLUENCERS

The problems your influencers experience will vary from one person to the next. If we put ourselves in their shoes, though, we can make an educated guess that these problems might revolve around things like delivering high-quality content and value to their audience, monetizing their audience, or creating partnerships.

Solving an influencer's problem may sound like a daunting endeavor, but it doesn't have to be. For instance, I've established strong, ongoing relationships with influencers by introducing them to someone they've ended up hiring, such as developers or salespeople.

While we don't have to solve these influencers' problems with our content, one of the most common issues influencers face is the need to deliver value to their audience. This means if you have generated high-quality content, you can help them deliver that value.

If you find yourself in this scenario, send a personalized e-mail that says something like:

Hey, John.

I really loved your article about hiring. I've actually taken your first piece of advice about setting aside twenty minutes every day to send cold e-mails to prospects.

I just wanted to let you know I wrote a post about some article titles I tested and some surprising results I found about managing a marketing team. I know you're an expert on this, and I'd love to get your feedback. Do you mind if I send you the post?

Thanks,
Len

Let's break this e-mail down. The first thing I've done here is to create a *personalized message*. These e-mails take longer to write because they require background work, but it's worth it because they net better results.

This personalization is followed up with a compelling teaser. You're giving the recipient a reason to read the article.

Note that with this strategy, you're asking for feedback, which is a far cry from what most people ask for. The more common ask is, "Hey, will you share this on Facebook?" The unspoken message of that tactic is, "Hey, can I have free access to your audience?"

The e-mail we're using here sends a very different message. It says, "Hey, I value your expertise way more than I value quick access to your Facebook followers." You're asking for *expertise* rather than for promotion, and there is a massive difference between those two requests. Asking for insight and expertise is actually a bigger ask, but, in doing this, you're conveying a level of respect that most people simply don't when e-mailing an influencer.

The last part of this e-mail is: "Do you mind if I send it to you?" The impact of this question is huge. Asking for *permission* to send something, rather than just attaching or linking to it in the initial e-mail, changes the dynamic of both the e-mail and your relationship with its recipient. Rather than saying, "Here's twenty minutes of work for you to do," you're conveying your appreciation for someone's time and asking about their preference. This ask is also inherently tinier, because the only action the recipient need take is to respond with a yes or a no. In the moment, it almost takes more work to say no than to say yes. If someone says no to this query, they'll feel like they should explain themselves or provide an excuse. Saying yes makes the decision disappear for now.

GETTING YOUR CONTENT IN FRONT OF INFLUENCERS

Once your influencer says yes, one of two things will happen. First, the influencer will give you feedback on your content, which is fantastic! Now you have input from an accomplished insider who knows your market and how to create great content for them.

Not only that, but once an influencer has provided feedback, they're invested in the development of your content. They've helped you make this thing a reality, which means they want it to succeed!

The alternative is that the influencer won't provide feedback, but once again, your e-mail has still set you apart from most marketers. This means the chances are high they'll share your post anyway. I see this happen all the time.

All of this keeps coming back to the same basic point: doing just a little bit more work than everybody else nets dramatically different results. In doing this, you are like the old-school insurance agent who still visits customers with gifts in hand during the holiday season. You're the one with the black book of solid relationships and referrals, versus the young gun who spams everybody over e-mail, is constantly being distracted by the latest shiny marketing tactic, and ultimately quits within a year because he can't get any traction.

IS THIS WORKING?

Like content marketing, content promotion isn't a quick task. You have to give the strategy some time and effort, and you won't see huge numbers in the beginning. There are benchmarks you can look for along the way to ensure you're moving in the right direction.

The first things you'll notice are social media shares and links back to your content. After a while, you might notice the influencers you've been reaching out to are proactively sharing your content. This takes time. Remember, your influencers have a lot more to lose than you do. By sharing your content, these influencers are sticking their necks out on the line for you. This means you have to prove yourself and consistently deliver, which means consistently providing great content.

When influencers begin to support you, you'll start to see referral traffic rise. Over time, you'll see organic traffic picking up. Again, this is a slow process. As long as your traffic is increasing a little every month—even by 5 percent—you can rest assured you're moving in the right direction.

Success is your ultimate goal, whether it's through sales, leads, engagement, or something else. How quickly this happens varies from case to case, but there are a number of factors to take into consideration. If you already have a thriving business or a well-known product, there's a better chance you'll achieve your goals more quickly. If you're still in the process of introducing yourself to the market, you may not see real business results for a few months.

It can be a tough pill to swallow, which is why a lot of content marketers, consultants, and agencies won't actually tell you this. They'll promise fast results in order to get hired. The excuses for why these results *didn't* happen quickly will come down the line.

I'M BEING IGNORED!

If you did everything recommended in this chapter and are still hearing crickets, it's a good indicator you're doing something wrong. But don't fret. This is still valuable information to have, because it allows you to steer in a new, more productive direction! You now have the feedback necessary to improve and try something different.

Your job from here on is to figure out what's not working. If you're getting traffic, but not sales or leads, then you're probably not doing a good job of capturing e-mail addresses or actually selling to your e-mail list. If you're creating great content, but not getting any traffic, you probably aren't promoting well enough. If you're putting out content and some people are sharing it, but your traffic dies down quickly, it's probably an indicator that the content isn't valuable or high quality, because people are bouncing away from it.

Even silence is valuable feedback. Silence prompts you to look at what's not working and to try something new and different. Ultimately, the market decides if your content is good or bad, but it also tells you how to make it better.

CHAPTER FIVE

NURTURE YOUR AUDIENCE

Getting an audience is the hard part; keeping them is—or, at least *should* be—easier. Still, this is an area where many companies struggle.

Think of the content marketing process as a funnel. Your big, broad audience at the top of the funnel consists of people who might be interested in doing business with you, but haven't committed to anything quite yet. Down the funnel a bit are those who have already expressed interest in having a relationship with you, whether it's by signing up for your newsletter or following you on social media. Go a bit further down the funnel, and you'll find people who have been engaged with your business for a while. In other words, they're warm leads who have been nurtured. Further down the funnel still, you have very, very warm leads. After that are customers, and finally at the bottom of the funnel, are loyal, long-term customers.

It takes a lot to get people into your funnel in the first place. Once you have people there, you want to keep them, because getting people into the top of the funnel is typically the most expensive obstacle to overcome. *Depending on which study you look at, and which market you're in, acquiring a new customer can be anywhere from five to twenty-five times costlier than retaining an existing one.* Pre-existing customers are a huge—and often ignored—opportunity for long-term profitability.

There's an old adage in the advertising industry that it takes seven "impressions" before a customer notices or knows your business. In my experience, this isn't too far from the truth. Sometimes it's four and sometimes it's twelve, depending on the customer, audience, and campaign. But it's rarely one. This is an expensive reality, and because of all of the noise out there, it's only going to get worse.

In addition to being cheaper, it's also *easier* to sell to an existing customer. According to the book *Marketing Metrics* by Paul Farris, the probability of selling to a new customer is, on average, 5 to 20 percent. This is compared to a 60 to 70 percent probability of selling to an existing customer. But it also makes sense, since we're talking about selling to people who don't know us versus selling to people who already trust us, and to whom we've already delivered value.

E-MAIL SUBSCRIBERS ARE NOT THE ULTIMATE GOAL

It's strangely common to see companies that have a huge e-mail list, yet a relatively tiny number of paying customers. It's not that uncommon to speak to a company that has 50,000 e-mail subscribers and fewer than 1,000 paying customers. Nonetheless, their marketing goal is to get more e-mail subscribers they can nurture into customers. *What?* You already have access to 49,000 subscribers you can turn into customers! In a scenario like this, it makes little sense to establish a goal that revolves around obtaining even more e-mail subscribers. You already have an audience, and not only that, it's an audience comprised of—presumably—low-hanging fruit. This is a lot of potential business to overlook, yet so many companies do.

Remember, the ultimate long-term goal of content marketing is customers, not subscribers. Just as much as we want to think about how to appeal to an audience and get them in the door, we also need to understand how to take them through the customer lifecycle. This lifecycle involves the customer purchasing products or services and building as profitable a relationship as possible.

There's a certain amount of comfort in sticking to what we know rather than trying something different and challenging. By the time you've built an e-mail list of 50,000, you're clearly skilled at building e-mail lists. But, if you can't convert those e-mail subscribers into customers, you're not actually making money off them. When faced with that problem, you're programmed to think, "Oh, I need to get another 50,000 e-mail subscribers, because I know how to scale e-mail signups."

This is not the correct answer. Instead, you need to figure out how to turn those other existing subscribers into customers. Once you've cracked that code, every single bit of traffic you obtain after that point is going to be so much more valuable, because a higher percent will convert into paying customers.

If you can't move your audience down the funnel, you will still fail at content marketing, no matter how many people you've drawn into the top of your funnel. Trust is the vehicle for appealing to more customers, but it doesn't actually pay the bills. You have to do something with that trust once you've earned it. You have to deliver on that trust, you have to make your audience glad you've warranted their trust, and, eventually, you have to ask them to do business with you. Without this last step, you've accomplished nothing.

MARKETING AND PUBLISHING ARE NOT THE SAME THING

When marketing and sales strategies are built around

traffic goals, it makes sense that you will start to adopt mistaken tunnel vision around e-mail subscribers and social followers. When that becomes the metric by which a project's success is determined, the people in charge of content marketing are incentivized to focus on only that one metric. Unfortunately, this metric is inherently flawed because nothing guarantees subscribers will become customers. Content marketing is not about broadcasting and building an audience—that's just a means to a greater end.

If you want to invest solely in audience-building, you're joining a breed of businesses that has been trying to do this for many years without much success. I assure you this is not a club you want to join. There are plenty of companies that have been built on developing great content, which has earned them armies of readers, and they've *still* failed, because they're built on content, not content *marketing*. A lot of people forget the second word of the phrase "content marketing." Marketing is the process of obtaining leads and sales for your business, *not* readers or traffic. For as much as we've discussed them throughout the book, the end goal isn't really even trust or authority. Those are just byproducts of doing content marketing correctly—conduits to the end goal, which is money in the door. It's paying customers we want.

To be successful at content marketing, you must have a firm understanding of how to get your audience to open their wallets not just once, but to continue buying from you and also refer others. To do this, you need to create content for every stage of the funnel, not just the top. After all, why would these newbie audience members trust you enough to give you their hard-earned cash? A lot of companies shoot themselves in the foot by gearing their web presence and in-person sales to giving the prospect only three choices: you can buy, not buy, or leave. Those are your options. To buy right out of the gate is a huge ask. If you make a huge ask upon first meeting someone, most people will say no. If they say no and walk out the door, you've lost them. You have to fight to get them back, and there are no guarantees that will be possible.

MOVING YOUR AUDIENCE THROUGH THE FUNNEL

Someone who stumbles into a helpful piece of content you've created may very well not be ready to buy from you immediately. But if your content proves valuable to them, then subscribing to your e-mail list to receive even more valuable content should be a compelling proposition. *That's* a more reasonable and realistic ask, with a much greater chance of success.

Once these potential customers are on your e-mail list, you can reach them with strong, high-value content that will build even more trust, thus sifting them further down the funnel. When someone gives you their e-mail address, they are giving you permission not just to send them content, but also to nurture your relationship and offer them your product or service.

GETTING SUBSCRIBERS

Sometimes called "lead magnets," opt-in bonuses are one of the most effective ways to get e-mail list subscribers. You've definitely seen this, likely in the form of an offer that says something like, "Download our free e-book." All you have to do to get this e-book is enter your e-mail address. This incentive makes you more likely to sign up than a simple "Sign up for our list!" offer would.

The more valuable and targeted your incentives are, the higher your conversion rate—the number of people who complete the action you're asking them to take—will be. Depending on your industry and audience, a standard offer that just asks for an e-mail subscription without the opt-in bonus might generate anywhere from a 1 to 2 percent conversion rate, if it's good. I regularly see these rates jump to 4 to 6 percent, simply by adding an opt-in incentive.

You can push these numbers even higher with a little bit of testing and experimentation. For example, Groove published a series of blog posts with seventeen e-mail scripts designed to grow a business. These e-mail scripts were for everything from hiring people to asking for discounts on software to communicating with customers during times of crisis. We shared these scripts as images so readers could screenshot them or use them as inspiration—but they couldn't copy and paste them.

Even as images, these scripts were valuable, but we knew they would be *more* valuable if they were in a simple text format that users could copy and paste. So, as an opt-in incentive, we offered a free PDF download that included the scripts in an easy copy-and-paste format. (When an opt-in bonus is highly targeted to a specific piece of content like this, it's called a "content upgrade.") The conversion rate on this new form was 22 percent! More than one of every five readers willingly shared their e-mail address with us. All it took was little bit of thinking about how to upgrade our content's value.

NURTURING EXISTING SUBSCRIBERS

Once you have e-mail subscribers and social media followers, you must nurture them to move them down the funnel toward a sale. This doesn't mean you should immediately try to sell them. In fact, in much of the testing I've done and researched, a sales pitch in a welcome e-mail is almost always going to perform worse than one that comes at the end of a sequence of nurturing e-mails.

Nurture sequences, sometimes called autoresponders or drip campaigns, are simple to set up. Nearly all e-mail service providers offer this functionality. Whatever your provider happens to call this feature, it's simply a sequence of e-mails that are automatically sent to new subscribers at timed intervals. For example, the first e-mail might be sent immediately, the second one a couple of days later, the third a couple of days after that, and so on. Your autoresponder is the hardest-working marketer on your team. It will send the same e-mail sequence thousands of times, which means your first subscriber, hundredth subscriber, and thousandth subscriber will all have the exact same experience, with zero additional work on your part.

All that's left is for you to set up your nurture sequence.

You can optimize autoresponders for years—and good marketers do—but even a simple one will drastically improve your results if you're beginning without one. To get started, just create a set of straightforward e-mails that look something like the following.

SAMPLE EMAIL SCRIPTS

Email #1

This initial welcome e-mail should be sent immediately upon subscription. It's a warm, personal thank you for signing up to your list. Express your gratitude for the subscriber's attention and let them know you understand how valuable their time is. Let them know what to expect now that they've signed up for your list.

Finally, include what I consider to be the most important part of this e-mail: a simple question that's easy to answer. This can be something along the lines of, "Why did you sign up for this list?" or "What are you struggling with most right now?" The answers will provide you with invaluable insights that serve as customer research for new content. These subscribers are extremely qualified to provide you with information, because they have proven they're interested in building a relationship with you. They can tell you what triggers caused them to sign up, so you can improve your content and opt-in incentives to focus on those triggers.

I find these answers fascinating, because it's not unusual to learn that your old assumptions about "conversion triggers" are wrong. In other words, what you are pitching as the main benefit of doing business with you may not be what the customer sees as the biggest benefit. Likewise, what you suspect to be their pain may not be their actual pain. Many companies fill up their content production calendar for months or even years using the feedback they've gleaned from these simple questions.

Here's an example of an effective welcome e-mail used at Groove:

Hey [first name],

I really appreciate you joining us at [your company name], and I know you'll love it when you see how easy it is to [explain what your product does].

We built [your company] to [your purpose], and I hope that we can achieve that for you.

If you wouldn't mind, I'd love it if you answered one quick question: why did you sign up for [your company]'s e-mail list?

I'm asking because knowing what made you sign up is really helpful for us in making sure that we're delivering on what our users want. Just hit "reply" and let me know.

By the way, over the next couple of weeks, we'll be sending you a few more e-mails to help you get maximum value from [your company]. We'll be sharing some tips, checking in with you, and showing you how some of our customers use [your company] to [your purpose].

Thanks,

[your name]

Email #2

After your welcome e-mail, you want to follow up with three to five more value-based e-mails.

The goal of these additional e-mails is to continue providing value, building trust, and demonstrating that you're committed to keeping and respecting your customers' attention. This helps your reader build the habit of opening your e-mails, because they expect something valuable each time.

The simplest way to do this is to solve one burning challenge in each e-mail. Simply send a piece of content every few days. This can be existing content that your new customer has never seen before.

Hi there,

Since launching the blog, we've published more than [insert number] posts on [insert subject matter].

To make it easier for you to get started, I put together a list of the most popular, valuable, and controversial blog posts we've ever published. These are the ones I still get the most e-mails about, even though some of them are more than a year old.

You can find those posts here: [insert blog link]

Hope you enjoy.

Cheers,

[your name]

Email #3

Hi there,

Today, I want to share some content I wrote that I think you'll find really valuable, but that's never appeared on our site.

I'm talking about guest posts I've written for blogs like [insert website name] and [insert website name]. You can check them out here:

[insert website address]

Thanks for reading, and I hope these posts are helpful to you!

Cheers,

[your name]

Email #4

Hi there,

Over the past week, I've sent you a series of e-mails to welcome you to the [insert your company name] community. I hope they've been valuable to you. This is the final e-mail in our Welcome Series.

If you're enjoying our blog, then I've got one more thing I want to tell you about that I think you'll find useful.

It's the reason we do everything we do at [insert your company name], and easily the most valuable thing we produce.

It's a tool that helps you [insert succinct product description with emphasis on how it helps the reader's company].

And to thank you for being a subscriber, I want to give you an extended 30-day free trial to give [insert product] a try, risk-free.

Check it out here: [insert website link]

Enjoy, and once again, welcome to [insert company name].

Cheers,

[your name]

FUTURE EMAILS

Once you have established value and trust through your nurturing sequence, and your audience is in the habit of opening your e-mails, you should begin to introduce your product or service, if you haven't done so already. You should always continue to provide value and be thoughtful, but your audience is now primed for you to make an ask.

> ## BUILDING A RELATIONSHIP THAT LASTS
>
> Remember that this is an ongoing process. You don't want to make a single sale. That's not a relationship; that's a transaction. You want to build a lifelong partnership with your customers, and e-mail is a great way to facilitate this and usher your customer through the various stages of the funnel. That might mean sending out content that explains how users can get more out of your product or service, or interesting tutorials about how to up-level the value of your product or service. Maybe you want to use your content to steer your audience toward other products you have that will resolve the problems they're struggling with. Whatever the case may be, continue to focus on your customer's experience, and you will continue to successfully move your audience on down the funnel.

HOW OFTEN SHOULD YOU E-MAIL YOUR SUBSCRIBERS?

We've all been on the receiving end of e-mails we've found annoying, so I understand why so many people wonder how frequently they should e-mail their subscribers. My answer for both the nurturing sequence and *all* marketing e-mails is that quality is more important than cadence. In other words, you should e-mail people as often as you have something valuable to share.

This guideline leaves plenty of room to test and play with your e-mail timing. I promise, you're not going to break anything. Try sending your e-mails two days apart and see what happens. Then send them three days apart. Are there any changes? How about one day apart?

At Groove, we e-mailed our entire audience three times a week. Our open rates didn't change when we went from e-mailing once per week to twice per week, or from twice to three times a week. It's the high-quality content that keeps e-mail subscriptions and open rates stable, not the frequency with which they're sent.

Plenty of marketers prefer less frequent sends, so as not to annoy subscribers; companies establish hard-and-fast rules about maximum allotments of e-mails over a given period of time. However, there is no silver bullet; you just have to test for yourself and your audience. Start with the frequency you feel comfortable with, monitor your open and click rates, and test in whatever direction you want to go, all the while ensuring your content remains consistently and reliably valuable.

ANALYZING METRICS

Your e-mail metrics will arm you with important information, such as how many people actually pull the trigger and make a purchase based on what you send. Three metrics to keep a close eye on are click-through rate, open rate, and sales. The click-through rate is the percentage of people who click on something in your e-mail. Your open rate is the percentage of subscribers who open your e-mails. And sales, of course, is how many subscribers purchase something because of an e-mail that you send.

If you watch these three metrics, you can better understand how to improve your marketing results. Is your open rate lower than it should be? Then test different subject lines to improve it. Is your click-through rate suffering? Your e-mail content or call-to-action needs work. No sales? Try a different offer.

As with many metrics, average benchmarks for these vary widely depending on industry, audience, and circumstance. Average open rates tend to vary between 15 and 25 percent, while average click-through rates swing from 1.5 to 4 percent. Let's say, for example, you have a list of 100,000 people you haven't emailed in the last two years. If you decide to start sending content again, you're guaranteed to see a lot of unsubscribes initially, because they've forgotten who you are and why they subscribed originally. If you're starting from day one with a list of zero and getting only subscribers who are really engaged, and you're actively *keeping* them engaged, your unsubscribe rate will be low.

On the topic of unsubscribe rates, here's something that might surprise you: unsubscribes aren't a bad thing. Yes, you read that correctly. Here's why: Email service providers charge based on the number of people on your list. If someone unsubscribes because they were never going to buy from you anyway, that's a *good* thing. They've unburdened you because you no longer have to pay for them.

Yes, I know this is a positive spin, but it's also realistic. A lot of people take an emotional hit from seeing people unsubscribe from their e-mail list; their feelings get hurt. This is a good time to remember we're in the business of selling, not publishing. You want your subscribers to consist of people who are going to buy from you.

As with unsubscribe rates, we can also benefit from looking at open rates in a different way than most people do. If you send an e-mail to a list of one hundred subscribers and have an open rate of 25 percent, that means twenty-five people opened your e-mail. But the perspective that many people miss is the flip-side: seventy-five people *did not* open your e-mail and have no idea what's inside. You can get disheartened about that wasted effort, or you can do something clever about it.

What if you took forty-five seconds to come up with a new, more compelling subject line, and sent those seventy-five people the same content again? This time, another twenty people open your e-mail. Now you're looking at a 45 percent rather than a 25 percent open rate, with less than a minute of work! Looking at metrics as opportunities rather than merely feedback, will empower you to refine, experiment, and get better.

CONTINUE HOLDING YOUR CUSTOMERS' HANDS

Content marketing is a powerful way to improve your customers' experience and build relationships that leave them truly looking forward to hearing from you. When you've achieved more than just a transactional relationship, your customers will *want* your insight. They value you and know you'll steer them in the right direction.

There's a regional grocery store near my house that I used to pop into every now and then. One day, I walked in looking for coconut milk. I found an employee mopping the floor in the produce aisle and asked if he could point me in the right direction. He looked at me and shrugged his shoulders, expressionless. "I don't know," he muttered. It was a jarring experience—not to mention my *last* experience at that store—but not dissimilar to how a lot of businesses treat their customers online.

Let's compare this to the experience of shopping at Whole Foods. If you ask an employee for assistance there, they are trained not just to tell you where a product is, but to *show* you where it is. Many of their stores don't even have aisle numbers for the express reason that Whole Foods doesn't want their employees to tell you that the coconut milk is in aisle six. On the other hand, aisle-numbering is a strategy that mega-supermarkets use because it saves them money and resources by allowing employees to wave you in the right direction. This makes life easier for the employee and the company, but not for the customer.

At Whole Foods, employees will stop what they're doing, climb down the ladder, and say, "Of course, come with me!" They will then walk you to the product, pick it off the shelf, and place it in your hands. *This* is how you should think about your online customer experience. You want to digitally walk people to their solution and hand it to them. You can do that with content from the very first encounter through the rest of your long and happy relationship.

CONCLUSION

THE PAY-OFF

I was invited to deliver a keynote speech at a conference run by a marketing company called Curaytor. Curaytor offers a much-loved product that helps its customers—mostly real estate agents at the time—create websites and bring their content marketing into the digital era.

The morning of my talk, I wandered around the conference floor and talked to attendees. I've been to a lot of conferences, so I thought I knew what to expect. I did not. This experience was unlike any I could remember. Everyone in attendance was already a paying Curaytor customer. That's not what was remarkable, however. What *was* remarkable was that I had never been to a conference where attendees so unanimously gushed about the host company. They couldn't say enough about how valuable Curaytor was, what great content they published, and how they steadfastly helped their customers with every problem they had. "I wouldn't be in business without their help," more than one attendee told me proudly. I should also say that Curaytor didn't fly these customers out for the conference as a freebie. Attendees paid between $500 and $1,000 just to attend, not including travel expenses to Orlando.

Toward the end of the show, Curaytor's co-founders, Chris and Jimmy, got onstage and were greeted with thunderous applause. They profusely thanked everyone for being there, then said they had an announcement to make. Chris and Jimmy went on to tell the audience they had been working on a new effort, a "done-for-you" marketing service that would serve a select group of their clients.

They explained that the service was just a prototype with a small team in place to test the approach, so they couldn't take on a lot of work to start. They needed twenty-five clients to sign up to test the new service, which would cost $15,000 a year. Chris and Jimmy assured their audience they had worked really hard on setting up this agency, but were also totally upfront about the fact that this was an entirely untested new program.

When the co-founders asked if anyone was interested, the audience went wild. People could not raise their hands fast enough, and the program sold out in minutes to the tune of $1.2 million in sales. Even though the product was new, Curaytor had already established incredible trust with their customer base. Now, remember: this audience didn't consist of representatives from Fortune 500 companies with the benefit of expense accounts. These were real estate agents paying for things out of their own pockets. But for them, it was an easy decision. They *knew* the product would be high quality. They knew it would offer a tremendous benefit to them.

Curaytor made more than $1 million in sales within five minutes of pitching this product to their preexisting customers.

This is the kind of customer relationship that most businesses would kill for. Curaytor didn't do anything magical to obtain this; there was no sorcery involved. They didn't do anything you can't do. They just followed the formula of being valuable, interesting, unique, and useful to their audience.

You can start becoming all these things today. If you're already creating content, step back and take an honest look at it. Is it solving problems? Is it delivering value? Is it meaningful, or is it just promotional?

These are simple questions, but all too often we do things because we think we're *supposed* to do them, rather than thinking through *why* we're doing them. In fact, just this one little question—*why?*—is enough to completely reframe how we do what we do. So many people start content marketing because they're "supposed to." It's just another checkbox.

The fix isn't easy, but it's simple. You will have to do the work to figure out how to do better content marketing. That begins with opening up a dialogue with your customers. I challenge you to have a real conversation with three to five customers this week. Ask them how they feel you're doing. What can you do to help them with their struggles and pains? If they had a magic wand and could solve any problem under the sun, what would it be?

This is how you start the process of uncovering the topics that will fuel great content. This is how you start the process of growing your business so that, just like Groove, Curaytor, Johnson & Johnson, Michelin, General Mills' Betty Crocker, and all other companies that win with exceptional content marketing, you are indispensable to your customers.

ACKNOWLEDGMENTS

Thanks first and foremost to my wife, Janina, for encouraging me to pursue this project, and for tolerating my constant and restless stomping around the house while I worked on it.

To my parents, Gail and Igor, and brother, Max, for supporting me longer than anyone else.

To Alex, Jordan, Lesley, and the rest of my extraordinary former teammates at Groove, the testing ground where I learned so much of what I share in this book.

To Nikki, for helping me share these lessons in a far more coherent manner than I would have on my own. To Greg, for his always sharp, thoughtful—and, yes, "clinical"— feedback. To Todd, who always expected more of me than I did of myself. To Tad and Julian, who showed me what it meant to write for people.

And to countless others for the incalculable value they've added to this book. I could fill an entire second book with the names of those who have helped me in my career, whether through advice and encouragement or simply by teaching me invaluable lessons through their own content marketing. But in the interest of brevity, this short list will have to do. I hope you all know who you are, and I hope you all know how much I appreciate you.

ABOUT THE AUTHOR

LEN MARKIDAN is the Chief Marketing Officer at Podia, a content marketing strategist, and a speaker. He has spent the past fifteen years as the brains behind successful content marketing strategies for a wide range of clients, from high-growth start-ups to Fortune 500, 100, and 50 companies, including Prudential, Jet.com, Groove, Mutual of Omaha, Chegg, Groupon, and Healthline. Len's work has been featured in *Forbes* and *Entrepreneur*. Learn more at lenmarkidan.com.

Printed in Great Britain
by Amazon